TO BED ... OR ELSE!

Ewa Lipniacka
Illustrated by Trish Hill

CELEBRATION PRESS
Pearson Learning Group

Asha and Hannah were friends and neighbors—
the best of friends and the best of neighbors.

They shared a birthday.

They shared their books.

They even shared their toys . . .

. . . most of the time.

Their moms were also friends and they shared, too. They shared their children.

If Hannah's mom had to go out in the evening, Hannah stayed with Asha.

And if Asha's mom had to work late, Asha moved in, with just a few of her things, to stay at Hannah's.

But the more they were together, the noisier they became.

And Hannah's mom just could not get them to bed.

She read them a story . . .

and another . . .

and another.

She sang songs until her throat was sore,

cast shadows on the wall until she was weak,

and still they would not sleep.

So then she got very angry.

"That's it!" she thundered.

"By the time I count to three, you two are in
bed, asleep. Dreaming the sweetest of dreams . . .
OR ELSE!!!"

"OR ELSE—what?" asked Asha and Hannah, together.

"ONE!" yelled Hannah's mom, and she even
slammed the door behind her.

"What does your mommy do for OR ELSEs, Hannah?"

"She usually just shouts a lot," said Hannah.

"That's not bad enough for an OR ELSE," declared Asha.

"OR ELSEs are much, much worse than that."

"She might put us in the trash can."

"She could give all your toys to a rummage sale. That's a really mean OR ELSE."

"TWO!"

"She might never, ever, buy us ice cream
again . . . and give us horrible medicine instead."

"TWO-AND-A-HALF!"

"Hannah, can she do magic OR ELSEs?
Could she turn us into frogs?"

"TWO-AND-THREE-QUARTERS!"

"What if she baked us in a pie and ate us all up?"

"She wouldn't, would she?" said Hannah.

"She just might," worried Asha, "and then
I would never see my mommy again."

"TWO-AND-SEVEN-EIGHTHS!"

"Hannah, I'm scared. I don't think I like OR
ELSEs."

"Me neither."

"Let's go to sleep—very, very quickly."

"Yes, let's."

And believe it or not—they did.

"Peace at last," thought Hannah's mom, as she cleared up the mess and tucked them in.

"Another lucky escape ..."

"I just don't know what I would have done if they hadn't gone to sleep!"

And between you and me, she doesn't ever, EVER, want to find out!